Philippine Heering
Fetze Pijlman

The Grebe

Mills & Boon, Limited
London · Sydney · Toronto

There is a wind blowing making the water rough on the middle of the lake. By the shore the water flows gently through the reeds. The small grebe are still covered in soft downy feathers and are easily swept away in a strong gust of wind. This is why they try to climb on top of something, usually father's or mother's back. They push against the sides of the mother grebe, squeaking, but they cannot climb on here. She is lower at the back and they manage to struggle on there.

It is safe and warm amongst her feathers. She floats off, away from the rough water.

Where the ditch starts the water is calm. Water lilies are flowering and flies buzzing. The eldest of the young grebe slides down into the water.

Father breaks the surface of the water. He has caught a small roach.

The young grebe cannot see very much yet. Sometimes they swim after a floating clump of reeds thinking it is their mother. Mother keeps a careful watch. A gust of wind moves the reeds – or is it something else? Nervously she pecks at her wing. She holds a small feather in her beak. The young swim towards her squeaking, thinking she has some food. The fastest bird gets hold of the feather with difficulty and swallows it. It is such hard food. The grebe swim past the reeds, catching insects. Suddenly there is a movement amongst the reeds. Mother screeches and the horrible noise travels across the water causing the young birds to hurry towards her. But a weasel has already caught one of them and he hurries off, holding the young grebe in his mouth.

The young grebe grow quickly, the eldest even faster than the other two. He is always there first when there is anything to eat.

But he still has difficulty in diving. At first he cannot manage at all. No matter how hard he tries, he can only get his head underwater. Gradually he realizes that he has to press his feathers against his sides so that the air is forced out.

He struggles and attempts an enormous dive. But after half a yard he shoots up again, just as fast.

He keeps practising, managing to stay underwater for longer and longer periods, getting better each time. Now he can easily catch a roach.

The young grebe now goes his own way. From time to time his mother or father still give him food, but when he begs they chase him away.

They have no time for him or the other young grebe now. Three new eggs have hatched in the nest and there are three hungry beaks asking for food.

The autumn brings rain. The grebe is now almost fully grown. Already he has a slight collar around his neck. But he has problems. There are few insects left and the fish are big or have already been eaten. There is frost and snow coming and the grebe must leave before the water freezes.

The grebe of the lake gather together to move away. They are heading for the coast. The frost has set in and the birds look for open water. The water has not quite frozen over by a lock on the way to the sea. The grebe lands here while the others fly on. Wild duck, crested duck, a merganser – they all share the same patch of water. They are a hungry group for there is hardly any food to be caught. But the birds do not quarrel. They keep as still as they can so that their oil does not dry up for this will protect them against the bitter cold.

The sun shines on the water of the lake. Some pilewort is already flowering amongst the young reed shoots. The grebe have returned. Winter was like a bad dream and they are all starving. The young grebe is there with them. Now he can dive with lightning speed, catching stickleback and eels. Once he has eaten his fill he takes time to groom himself. He pecks the vermin from his feathers and then rolls over, letting the water flow off his back. The collar on his neck slowly grows wider to form a really large grebe collar and he develops a beautiful crest on his head.

He feels the sun shining on him and he is so pleased with his new feathers that he shows them off to all the other grebe. He swims along holding up his head and then glides underwater without disturbing the surface. When he comes up he sees a female grebe. She looks as if she is made of silver, her feathers shine so. He would like to approach her.

The young grebe swims by the female. His crest stands up in excitement. When he swims past again he shakes his head with delight and she shakes hers back. He calls out to her and she calls back. They keep on playing this game, swim-ming past each other and shak-ing their heads.

Then he swims straight towards her. The female does not move aside but presses against him and he pushes back. They rush towards each other, climbing higher and hig-

her out of the water. Now and then they pause. Then the game starts again and each time they play it a little differently. They have grown attached and build a small island with reeds and leaves; this is all part of their game. When the island is

finished they begin to shake their heads again and swim against each other. Then they go to the island. This game is so wonderful! The male shakes and dances on the water while the female grebe sits watching on the island.

The nest is soft and soggy – a bed of reeds with a border around it. The female has laid four white eggs. She sits on them for many hours, the soft down of her front keeping them warm.

After a while she becomes hungry. The male relieves her so that she can go and look for food. She must also make sure that no other birds swim into their territory.

There is much life on the lake now: the duck is swimming around with her young, the water hen is broody and the frog is croaking – he is looking for a female to court. Meanwhile, the young grebe are growing inside their eggs. The soggy plants in the nest are soft and warm and they rot slightly so that the eggs are even safer. Slowly the eggs turn to the colour of the nest.

The grebe is sitting on the nest when suddenly he hears people approaching. He must take flight.
Quickly, he uses his feet to push some of the reeds over the eggs and he slips into the water. He makes sure that the nest is well hidden and then dives under.
At a safe distance he surfaces. Keeping only his head above

the water, he can see everything.
The people walk towards the
nest. The grebe pretends that
nothing has happened and he
swims about, pecking at his
feathers.

The grebe keeps a close watch
on the people as they walk past
the nest. When the danger is
past he returns but, just to be
sure, he takes a detour.

The four week brooding period is nearly over. Life has already begun in the eggs and slight noises can be heard.

Then the mother grebe feels a knocking inside an egg and she gets up to take a look. One of the eggs has a small crack in it. Then all is quiet. The mother sits down again because the other eggs must be kept warm. After hours of incubating the eggs a small piece of shell finally breaks off. The crack gradually widens. The head of the young bird pokes out and the sticky little body frees itself from the shell.

The mother grebe starts to clear up the mess. By now the second egg has a small crack.

The mother grebe has gone for a swim with the young birds. Father sits on the eggs looking at them occasionally to see how number two is doing.
The young bird manages to struggle out of its egg sur-prisingly quickly. From the edge of the nest he tries to climb on to his father's back. Already, his feathers are drying in the sun. When he is finally sitting on his father's back he has a short rest. Suddenly a rat appears. Father

grebe is half asleep and suddenly starts. With one move he
sticks his head out threa-
teningly at the rat. His collar
stands up straight.
But the small grebe has nothing
to hold on to and falls into the
water.

But there is nothing the grebe can do. He must return to the nest to protect the eggs. The young grebe squeaks. His feathers are not yet dry and he starts to sink.

Mother grebe rushes to the commotion at great speed. Seeing the ball of feathers floating on the water, she dives down and surfaces directly under the young bird. Now she has two young grebe between her wings.

The grebe look to see if the young bird is injured. It is squeaking, hoping to get something to eat. Everything is alright.

The sun has set and the moon has risen. It is peaceful on the lake but not yet quiet. The frogs are croaking as hard as they can and everywhere ducks are quarrelling.

The third young grebe is now emerging from its egg, but it is taking a long time to appear. The grebe are busy all night long. It is only when the moon has almost gone down that the

young bird manages to free itself and falls asleep on mother's back.
The grebe bobs about on the water. He catches whatever flies by him, a water beetle or a dragonfly, and he takes it to his young.
Tired, he tucks his beak between his feathers and falls asleep.

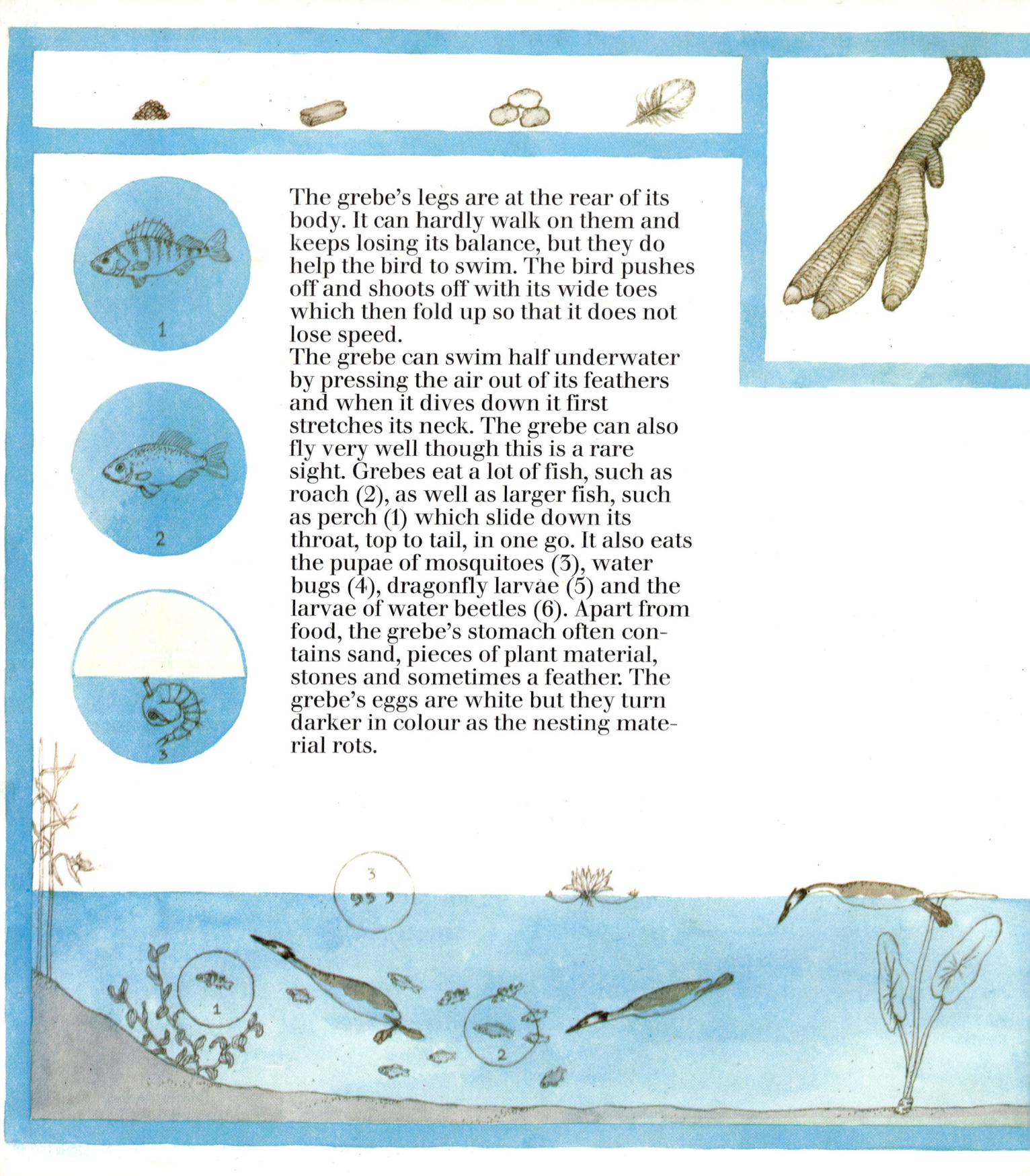

The grebe's legs are at the rear of its body. It can hardly walk on them and keeps losing its balance, but they do help the bird to swim. The bird pushes off and shoots off with its wide toes which then fold up so that it does not lose speed.

The grebe can swim half underwater by pressing the air out of its feathers and when it dives down it first stretches its neck. The grebe can also fly very well though this is a rare sight. Grebes eat a lot of fish, such as roach (2), as well as larger fish, such as perch (1) which slide down its throat, top to tail, in one go. It also eats the pupae of mosquitoes (3), water bugs (4), dragonfly larvae (5) and the larvae of water beetles (6). Apart from food, the grebe's stomach often contains sand, pieces of plant material, stones and sometimes a feather. The grebe's eggs are white but they turn darker in colour as the nesting material rots.